Debbie Duncan's books are a *
directly into our anxious cultui
through the lens of emotion, in ....
The brilliant, two-tiered approach means that both little
ones and older children alike will come away with a greater
grasp of their emotional and mental well-being.

Katharine Hill, *UK Director of Care for the Family*

Adults and children will find this series thought-provoking
and encouraging in exploring how we deal with feelings.
We often hide from negative emotions, so books that help
children face them, and talk and pray about them, are an
invaluable resource to promote emotional well-being.

Sue Monckton-Rickett, *Chair of the Association of Christian Counsellors*

Despite the increased focus on mental well-being around us,
we rarely consider the emotional challenges of characters in
the Bible. And yet, their feelings and responses are so helpful
for us as we navigate our own obstacles and opportunities.
This series gives parents and adults the tools to dig deeper
with children and young people, enabling them to relate
and learn from the valuable truths and experiences found in
these much loved stories. These books will build emotional
resilience and strong faith – and are great fun to read.
What's not to love?

Cathy Madavan, *Speaker, author, and Kyria Network board member*

Debbie Duncan's *God Cares* series brilliantly helps children understand the emotions of Bible characters while encouraging them to explore their own emotions in the face of similar situations. What is more, the books do it in a style that retains the excitement and adventure of the stories themselves. The books also offer practical help to parents and carers as they engage with their children on this voyage of discovery.

Bob Hartman, *Author and performance storyteller*

According to Barnardo's, one in ten children have a diagnosable mental health condition and many, while they are undiagnosed, are unhappy and anxious for many reasons in today's world. Early intervention is vital before their feelings become more problematic. Debbie's *God Cares* series offers a gentle in-road for parents and carers to encourage them to open up about what they are feeling and what is going on in their lives. Learning early on how much God loves them and cares for them can only be a positive. Seeing their own feelings in well-known Bible characters will show them that no matter what the circumstance, God always wins!

Karen Lennie, *Cognitive Behavioural Psychotherapist PG Dip, BABCP Member (Accred)*

GOD CARES

WHEN LIFE IS UNFAIR

Joseph and
Other Stories

By Debbie Duncan

CANDLE
BOOKS

This book is dedicated to Malcolm, a child at heart
whose life at times has mirrored that of Joseph's.
You have taught me so much about God – thank you.

Samuel – I thought you would enjoy this book.
May you grow up knowing Jesus loves you.

And thank you to Josh. Thank you for sharing your
thoughts with us and remember God is always with you.

Text copyright © 2021 Debbie Duncan
This edition copyright © 2021 Lion Hudson IP Limited

The right of Debbie Duncan to be identified as the author of this work has been asserted
by her in accordance with the Copyright, Designs and Patents Act 1988.

Published by
Lion Hudson Limited
Wilkinson House, Jordan Hill Business Park
Banbury Road, Oxford OX2 8DR, England
www.lionhudson.com

ISBN 978 1 78128 401 8

First edition 2021

Acknowledgments
Cover illustration by Anita Belli.
Scripture quotations taken from the Holy Bible, New International Version Anglicised.
Copyright © 1979, 1984, 2011 Biblica, formerly International Bible Society. Used by
permission of Hodder & Stoughton Ltd, an Hachette UK company. All rights reserved.
"NIV" is a registered trademark of Biblica. UK trademark number 1448790.
p.6 quotation taken from *Aspire* magazine.

A catalogue record for this book is available from the British Library

Printed and bound in China, February 2021, LH54

CONTENTS

About the Series

> *"In raising healthy children, it's not enough to just focus on the physical aspect of health. To be truly healthy, a child's emotional health must be nurtured and strengthened. Developing a mental attitude of wellness is also essential. When we adopt an attitude of wellness, we take on a belief that being well is a natural, normal state."*

Jane Sheppard, "A Wellness Approach for Children", *Aspire* magazine, 9 June 2009

The *God Cares* series is about providing parents with a biblical approach to discussing emotions and behaviour with their children to provide an attitude of wellness. Children of different ages and at different stages of their emotional development approach things differently, so this series works on two separate levels: **readers aimed at five- to seven-year olds, and chapter books aimed at children aged eight and above**. Please note that children progress at different rates in terms of their reading ability and emotional development, so the age ranges are only a guide for parents and carers.

The Bible stories are retold reflecting on the emotions. Children are encouraged to discuss this and relate the stories to their own situations. Sections at the back provide a reflective space for children, and practical advice for parents and carers.

About the Author

Debbie Duncan, the author of *The Art of Daily Resilience* and *Brave*, is a nurse, a lecturer, the mother of four grown-up children, and the grandmother of Arthur and Caleb. Debbie has considerable insight into what constitutes resilience and bravery: the ability to cope, to stay on course, and to bounce back. In her books she considers what is required for physical, mental, and spiritual durability, interweaving biblical teaching and prayers with personal anecdotes and sound advice. This she now applies specifically to support parents and carers raising children.

Introduction

The Bible was written many hundreds of years ago. God used different people to write it but they were inspired by or helped by God. That is why, even today, the stories and parables in it help us to make sense of the world we live in. We can also learn from the history and life stories of different characters in the Bible.

Throughout these pages, we will learn about the life of Joseph. We are told about his story in the book of Genesis, which is the first book of the Bible. Joseph was one of twelve brothers. His father loved him but his brothers were jealous of him and ended up hating him. Throughout Joseph's life, bad things kept happening to him even though he just wanted to help people. He was thrown into a pit, sold as a slave, accused of something he hadn't done, and put into prison and forgotten about. Life was unfair.

Joseph knew that despite all these awful things that kept happening to him, God was still with him. He knew he could trust God no matter what happened in his life. Joseph also teaches us that with God's help we can also forgive people who have hurt us. Joseph helped the baker and the cupbearer, and he helped Pharaoh (the king) by interpreting his dreams. At the end of the story, we learn that he forgave his brothers for what they had done to him. What an extraordinary man who trusted God even when life was unfair!

After reading the story, discuss it, and how you feel, with your parents or those who care for you. There are some talking points at the end of the book to help you.

CHAPTER ONE

LET'S MEET JOSEPH

Joseph lived in a land called Canaan in the country now called Israel. Joseph was the second youngest of the family. In fact, he was much younger than all but one of his brothers. For a while, he was the "baby" of the family. He had eleven brothers. They were called Reuben, Simeon, Levi, Judah, Dan, Naphtali, Gad, Asher, Issachar, Zebulun, and Benjamin. They had the same father, named Israel – like the country – but were from four different mothers. They were one large, messy, complicated family.

Joseph was his father's favourite son, which meant that his brothers were not treated in the same way as him. In fact, Joseph's brothers thought that their father spoiled Joseph and loved him more than them. Joseph was Israel's favourite son because his mother was Rachel, Israel's favourite wife. She had waited a long time before she was able to have Joseph, her first son. Later she had a second son named Benjamin.

Joseph's story begins when he was seventeen years old. He was out on a hillside in Canaan looking after his father's sheep with his brothers. There would have been a lot of sheep and keeping them safe was hard work. Joseph wasn't impressed by how his brothers looked after the sheep, and told his father so. Then Israel showed Joseph how much he loved him by buying him a fancy coat. It was made of rich materials of many colours. Joseph's brothers were jealous as they didn't get a new coat. This led to his brothers feeling angry about this unfair situation. They were very unkind to Joseph. They even hated him.

There is another man in the Bible whose family treated him differently. This man was called David and his story is told in the book of Samuel. Even though he was a shepherd boy, he later became a king of Israel. These events and even the songs David wrote fill many pages in the Bible. Like Joseph, he was also the youngest son with seven older brothers. The following story is about when David found out he would become the next king.

God told the priest Samuel to go to Bethlehem, find Jesse, and anoint one of his sons as the next king of Israel. Samuel went to Bethlehem and invited Jesse, David's dad, and his sons to a special ceremony. Samuel didn't tell them he was going to anoint the next king of Israel in case the reigning king heard and got angry with him!

Jesse arrived with his sons. Samuel looked at them and saw a tall, strong man. He was sure he was the one that God wanted to be king. However, God reminded Samuel that what was inside a person was more important than their appearance. Seven sons of Jesse walked past Samuel and God told him that none of them would be king. Then Samuel asked Jesse, "Are these all the sons you have?" Jesse replied that there was also the youngest son, David, but he was looking after the sheep.

David was sent for and stood in front of Samuel. Samuel anointed him with oil, a sign that God had chosen him for a great purpose.

This story can be found in the Old Testament in 1 Samuel 16.

Can you think of a time when things were very unfair, and you did not know what to do? Try writing down how you felt and share your thoughts with someone you trust.

This is space for you to write in.

CHAPTER TWO

JOSEPH'S DREAMS

One day, Joseph had a strange dream. He shared it with his brothers and they hated him even more. In the dream, Joseph and his brothers were collecting the wheat harvest they needed to make bread. The wheat harvest was stacked high like hay bales. Suddenly, Joseph's stack rose up and towered above his brothers' stacks. Their stacks bowed down to Joseph's.

Joseph then had another dream. This time, the sun, moon, and eleven stars bowed down toward

Joseph. He shared this with his brothers. They asked, "Do you intend to reign over us?" They hated Joseph even more. This time Joseph also told his father about the dream. His father told Joseph off. He said, "Will your mother and I and your brothers actually come and bow down to the ground before you?"

Joseph's brothers were angry, but his father went away and thought about what it could mean. Imagine how they and Joseph felt. Perhaps Joseph was proud or maybe he was not thinking about how his brothers must have been feeling – he had a lot to learn!

Joseph's brothers were out with the sheep one day. Israel asked Joseph to go and check on his brothers as they were far from home. The brothers were not where Joseph thought they would be, but a stranger pointed him in their direction. The brothers saw Joseph coming toward them from a distance as he was wearing his brightly coloured coat. They talked about how they could get rid of him.

"Here comes that dreamer!" they said to one another. They decided to capture him, kill him, throw him down a deep hole, and pretend a wild animal had eaten him. Reuben heard their plan and tried to stop them. He managed to persuade them not to kill Joseph but instead to throw him into an empty water pit. Secretly, Reuben wanted to rescue Joseph later. So the brothers ripped Joseph's fancy coat and threw him down into the pit. Then all the brothers apart from Joseph and Reuben had some dinner!

~~~~~~~~~~~~~~~~~~~~~~~~~~~~~~~~

Elijah was God's spokesperson to the people of Israel during a difficult time in their history. The people had stopped following God. King Ahab and Queen Jezebel worshipped other gods and are recorded as being the cruellest of leaders. The queen ordered the death of hundreds of prophets who spoke God's word. Elijah performed many miracles to show the people God's power but he was also afraid. He received a message from the king that he was going to be killed. Elijah ran away and hid. He was scared, worried, and felt alone. He probably felt a little like Joseph did in the pit.

Then an angel appeared to Elijah and told him to get up. He told Elijah where to go and even gave him bread and water for the journey. Elijah travelled for forty days to the mountain that was a symbol to the people of Israel of the presence of God. They called it Mount Horeb or the Mountain of God. On that mountain, God spoke to Elijah and reminded him that he was with him. God is with us in the lowest pit or on the highest mountain. He understands what we are going through.

This story can be found in the Old Testament in 1 Kings 19.

~~~~~~~~~~~~~~~~~~~~~~~~~~~~~~~~~

As Joseph's brothers were sitting eating their dinner, they saw a group of traders arrive on their camels. The camels were loaded up with spices and items to sell in Egypt. Judah saw them and had an idea for he no longer wanted to kill Joseph. He suggested that they could sell Joseph to the traders. That way they would get some money, they would not have to kill their brother, and Joseph would not be a problem anymore. So, the traders took Joseph away. Sometimes wrong or unfair situations happen, and they can lead to hurt and pain.

Reuben did not know what his brothers had done. He returned to the place where Joseph had been left and was upset to discover he was gone. There was nothing he could do. His brothers picked up Joseph's coat, covered it in animal blood, and took it back to their father. They lied. They asked their father if it was Joseph's coat. Israel recognized it and became very upset. He thought his son had been attacked and killed by a wild animal. Reuben could have told his father the truth but instead he didn't say anything. Their father cried for his lost son while Reuben was distressed that his plan hadn't worked out. Meanwhile, Joseph was sold as a slave in Egypt.

How do you think Joseph felt when his own brothers sold him as a slave? What do you do when things seem unfair? Pause for a moment to think about how God is listening and how he is always ready to hear our prayers.

Chapter Three

WRONGLY ACCUSED

Joseph was taken by the traders to Egypt where he was bought as a slave by Potiphar, the captain of the Egyptian guard. Joseph must have felt very alone and frightened – he was being sold as a slave to a stranger in a country he didn't know. He may not have spoken their language but he knew God was with him. Joseph could have been filled with anger and disheartened by the unfairness of his situation, but he did not show those feelings. He was humbled by his

position and worked hard, and God blessed
him.

Joseph's master saw that God was with
Joseph and this gave him success in everything
he did. In fact, Potiphar trusted Joseph and put
him in charge of his whole household. God blessed
Potiphar and his household because of Joseph.
Potiphar didn't have to worry about anything
because Joseph sorted out everything for him.
The only thing Potiphar had to do was decide
what he wanted to eat.

Now Joseph was handsome and Potiphar's wife
began to notice him. She decided she liked Joseph
and wanted to be more than a friend to Joseph.
She wanted him to be her boyfriend even though
she was married. Joseph refused. He told her that
it was wrong. He reminded her that Potiphar
trusted him and he could not break his trust.
Joseph knew he could not fail God.

One day, Joseph went into the house to do
his work but discovered that none of the other
servants were there. Potiphar's wife caught Joseph
by his coat and tried to kiss him. Joseph ran out
of the house leaving his coat behind him. He must
have been frightened as he was really trying to do

the right thing. Potiphar's wife called out to the servants and accused Joseph of trying to attack her. She made up the story and showed them Joseph's coat. Poor Joseph – he was in trouble again over another coat. Potiphar listened to his wife and believed her. He was very angry with Joseph for he had trusted him. Joseph was put in prison with Pharaoh's prisoners.

Life just seemed so unfair for Joseph. Here he was, thrown into another place he could not escape from, but Joseph knew God was with him, even in prison. Instead of being angry with God for allowing it to happen, Joseph trusted God. He didn't think about who was to blame. He decided to let go of the anger he felt toward Potiphar's wife and to do his best to improve the situation he found himself in. He chose to learn humility and serve those around him. Joseph trusted God for his future.

The warden of the prison saw that there was something special about Joseph. He put him in charge of all the other people in the prison. God blessed everything Joseph did and the warden didn't have to worry about anything.

Sometime later, Pharaoh's cupbearer and

Pharaoh's baker offended him, so he threw them in prison. The captain of the guard asked Joseph to take care of them. One night, both the cupbearer and the baker had a dream. The next morning, Joseph could see that the two men looked distressed. He was now aware of other people's feelings. He could see how unjust their situation was and wanted to help them. Joseph told them that God could interpret their dreams.

The cupbearer told Joseph about his dream first. In it there was a vine with three branches that flowered and produced grapes. The cupbearer took the grapes, squeezed them into Pharaoh's cup, and put the cup in his hand. Joseph told the two men that the dream meant the following: the three branches meant three days. In the next three days, Pharaoh would restore the cupbearer to his position.

Joseph asked the cupbearer to remember him when he was released. He told the cupbearer that he had been captured and taken from his home. Although he had done nothing wrong, he had been put in prison. Life was very unfair for Joseph.

The baker heard the good news that Joseph

had given the cupbearer and decided to ask Joseph to interpret his dream too. He told Joseph he dreamed he had three baskets of bread on his head. The basket on top had lots of baked goods for Pharaoh but the birds were eating them out of the basket. Joseph didn't give the baker a favourable interpretation of his dream. He told him that in three days' time, Pharaoh would have him killed.

Three days later, it was Pharaoh's birthday. He released the cupbearer and had the baker killed. The cupbearer did not remember what Joseph had said. Imagine how Joseph felt several days later when he was still in jail. The cupbearer had promised to tell people how Joseph had helped him, but he had forgotten him.

Jesus reminds us that we should be thankful when good things happen to us. Leprosy was a very common disease at the time when Jesus was alive. It was a nasty skin disease that meant you could lose the feelings in your hands and feet. People were scared of getting it. They did not understand the disease and called anyone who had it "unclean". Those who had leprosy were called lepers, and were forced to live in their own areas away from the people in the cities and towns. They could not stay with their families, have dinner with friends, or meet with others. They had to stay away from everyone.

One day, as Jesus was heading to Jerusalem, he entered a village where there were ten men who had leprosy. They stood at a distance, shouting to Jesus and asking him to heal them. Jesus told them to go to the priest in the Temple to show him they were clean and had no leprosy. As the men did that, they were instantly healed. However, only one of them came back to Jesus to thank him and God for the miracle. Jesus asked, "Were not all ten cleansed? Where are the other nine?"

Sometimes we can become so focused on what is wrong that we forget what is good. The cupbearer should have helped Joseph as Joseph had helped him.

This story can be found in Luke 17.

~~~~~~

Is there anyone that has helped you who you want to thank? Is there a kind gesture that you can show them? Thank God for what they have done for you.

~~~~~~

Joseph continued to wait patiently, serving God even in prison and trusting he was in control.

Two years later, Pharaoh woke up after having a strange dream. He dreamed that he was standing by the Nile, the main river in Egypt. Out of the water came seven fat, healthy cows. After them came seven skinny, awful-looking cows. The very skinny cows ate the fat cows and then the dream ended. He fell asleep again and dreamed that there were seven heads of wheat all growing from one stalk. After them grew another seven heads of grain, but they were thin and didn't look healthy. The thin heads ate the fat heads of wheat. What a strange dream!

Pharaoh was really confused about the dreams

and thought that his god was trying to tell him something. He ordered all his wise men in the palace to tell him what they meant but no one could. Then the cupbearer remembered Joseph and told Pharaoh about him. Pharaoh sent for Joseph, who had to have a wash after being in jail before he could enter the palace.

Have you ever felt forgotten or left out? Use the box on the next page to draw a picture in pencil of the last time you felt alone. After you have done this, add some colour showing where God was in this situation.

CHAPTER FOUR

JOSEPH BECOMES EGYPT'S GOVERNOR

Pharaoh sent for Joseph and told him that he had heard that he could interpret dreams. Joseph told Pharaoh that he could not do it but that his God could help him. What a brave thing to say! So Joseph listened to Pharaoh describing his dreams and trusted God to guide him.

Joseph told Pharaoh that the dreams meant the same things. He explained that there would be seven years of good harvest. Then there would be seven years of drought and famine. Joseph told Pharaoh that God had used the dreams to warn him of what would happen. He suggested that Pharaoh look for wise men to ensure that they keep one-fifth of the good harvest and store this away for the years of famine. Pharaoh thought that Joseph had a good plan but he did not know anyone who was wise enough to help. He told his officials that the wisest and godliest man he knew was Joseph. So Pharaoh put Joseph in charge of his palace. All the people of the land had to obey Joseph. Only Pharaoh was more important than him.

Pharaoh put a ring on Joseph's finger and a gold chain around his neck to signify his royal position. He also gave Joseph robes made from the best fabric. Joseph once again had fine robes on his back. He also married the priest's daughter. He had a chariot in which he rode around Egypt and all the people knew how important he was. At thirty years old, he held one of the highest positions in the land and the people did what he asked them to do. In the following seven years, Joseph stored up huge quantities of grain for the following years of famine. Everyone in Egypt had plenty to eat, even during the famine. People from other countries came to Egypt to buy grain from Joseph.

The famine was so bad that it also affected Canaan, where Joseph's family lived. His father had heard that there was grain for sale in Egypt. He decided to send his sons there to buy grain, although he kept Joseph's youngest brother, Benjamin, at home. The brothers travelled the long distance to Egypt and were brought before its governor, Joseph. He would have been in his late thirties now, and looked very different from the young seventeen-year-old brother they had thrown into a pit. He was a member of the royal household with robes, gold chains, a shaven face, and styled hair. He would even have had dark eye make-up around his eyes. No wonder his brothers didn't recognize him! However, Joseph recognized them immediately. He pretended to be a stranger, speaking harshly to them in Egyptian. An interpreter helped the brothers to understand what Joseph said.

How do you think Joseph felt when his brothers bowed before him? He remembered his dreams.

Joseph wanted to test his brothers to see if they were
sorry for what they had done to him. He wanted
to know whether they were still dishonest and full
of hate. Joseph accused them of being spies and the
men insisted they were innocent. They told Joseph
that they were twelve brothers – one was at home
with their father, and one was dead. Imagine how
Joseph felt hearing his brothers say he was dead.

Joseph demanded that the brothers return home
to fetch their youngest brother and bring him to
Egypt. Meanwhile, one of them would be kept in
jail. They had to prove they were honest. They
all began to talk to each other about what had
happened to Joseph in the past. Reuben told his
brothers that they should have listened to him and
that they were being punished for their crime. They
didn't realize that Joseph understood what they
were talking about.

Eventually, Simeon was kept as a prisoner and
the rest were sent to collect Benjamin. Before the
brothers left, Joseph ordered his servants to fill their
sacks with grain and to put each man's money
back into his sack. Joseph did this to test them. He
wanted to know what they would do when they
found the money.

The brothers travelled back to Canaan. At night, they stopped to rest. One of the brothers opened his sack to feed his donkey, and found his money. Then one by one, each brother checked his sack and saw his money in it. They were afraid they would be accused of stealing and wondered why God had allowed this to happen. Often, things happen to us that don't make sense. Sometimes bad things happen to good people – it is unfair, and we don't know why. The brothers wondered what they had done wrong and maybe they remembered what they had done to Joseph.

The brothers returned home to face their father and tell him what had happened. Israel was distressed. He had lost Joseph, Simeon was in prison in Egypt, and now the governor of Egypt wanted Benjamin. Reuben promised his father that he would bring Benjamin and Simeon back to him. Remember that although Reuben hadn't been part of the scheme to sell Joseph as a slave, he had still done a bad thing because he hadn't told their father what had happened. But now he had changed!

The brothers didn't rush back to rescue Simeon. In fact, they didn't plan to go back until they had nearly finished their grain. Judah also promised his father that they would take Benjamin as Joseph had requested, but that they would bring him and Simeon back safely. Although the brothers feared what could happen, they travelled to Egypt. They took double the amount of money and presented themselves to Joseph. When Joseph saw Benjamin, he told his men to take his brothers to his own house and prepare a meal for them. The brothers were puzzled. They told Joseph's servant about the money they had found in their grain sacks after their last visit, and offered to give it back. Joseph's servant told them not to worry. He freed Simeon and helped them to wash and change after their long journey.

When Joseph arrived, they all bowed before him with gifts. He asked them about their father and heard that he was still alive. He saw Benjamin and was so emotional that he had to find a place to cry. They had a feast at Joseph's house and were told to sit in order of age, from the youngest to the oldest. They must have wondered what was going on!

As the brothers prepared to leave, Joseph tested them again. Would they protect and look out for one another in an unfair situation? Once again, he ordered his men to hide the money in the brothers' sacks of grain, and also to put a silver cup in Benjamin's sack. The brothers had not travelled far when Joseph's men caught up with them and accused them of theft. They insisted they were innocent. However, the men told them that as the silver cup was in Benjamin's sack, he would be put in prison.

The group travelled back to Egypt. When the brothers arrived at Joseph's house, they fell on their knees and begged Joseph to be merciful to Benjamin. Judah told Joseph that they were innocent of stealing the money and the cup, but that they were guilty of other things. Judah offered to take Benjamin's place in prison, even though none of them had stolen anything. This was Judah, the brother who had come up with the idea of selling Joseph into slavery. He was now offering to become a prisoner himself instead of his brother.

Joseph saw how his brothers responded to the situation. They cared about their father and younger brother. They had even offered to be punished instead of Benjamin. Joseph could no longer disguise himself. He revealed himself to his brothers, and was excited at being reunited. Soon the whole of Egypt knew how excited he was but Joseph's brothers could not speak as they were so frightened of him.

Joseph again told his brothers who he was and that he had forgiven them. He knew that although it was unfair that he had been sold into slavery in Egypt, God had used this situation for good. Joseph had interpreted Pharaoh's dream and so they were prepared for the famine that had affected all the land. Joseph was now able to help his family and all the people of Israel. That is exactly what he did. We can only imagine how his father must have felt when he hugged his son – the one he had thought was dead. And Joseph must have been so thrilled to hug his father!

Jesus tells us in the Bible that we should try to forgive people who hurt us. This is because God forgives us. This is a better way to live. If we hold onto our unwillingness to forgive, it weighs us down. It makes us sad and even angry. God can help us to let it go. Jesus teaches us to ask for God's help to do this in the prayer he told us to pray. It's known as the Lord's Prayer, and you can find it in Matthew chapter 6, verses 9—13.

Use the space on the next page to write out the Lord's Prayer.

CHAPTER FIVE

WHAT YOU CAN DO

Learning about Joseph and his extraordinary life reminds us that even when things are difficult and life is unfair, we can trust God. I am sure there would have been many times when Joseph felt that he did not deserve the things that happened to him. He could have thought that life was unfair and blamed God for what happened to him. However, Joseph knew that God was with him when he was thrown into a pit, when he was captured and taken to Egypt, and even when people wrongly accused him of things he hadn't done. God blessed him and eventually he became second in command of Egypt – even in charge of Potiphar, the captain of the guard.

I had a friend help me with this book. He is a child like you called Josh Simmons. Josh loves reading. This is what he told me about the life of Joseph.

Joseph went into slavery and prison but still carried on believing in God. He kept praying even when it didn't look good! God used what happened to teach Joseph he could trust God. God uses the story of Joseph to teach us that we can trust him.

Talking Points

The following questions are here to help you think about the things we have read. They are ideas for you to chat about with your parents, a teacher, someone at church, or another adult you can trust.

Questions:

- How do you think Joseph felt about the way his brothers treated him?
- Do you have a brother or know someone like Reuben, Simeon, Levi, Judah, Dan, Naphtali, Gad, Asher, Issachar, Zebulun, or Benjamin? Do you think Joseph was afraid when he was in the dark pit?
- Do you think Joseph had an easy life as a slave?
- How do you think Joseph put God first when he was in prison?
- Do you think it was easy for Joseph to forgive his brothers?
- What makes you think Joseph's brothers had changed?

Our world is broken because of the wrong things we do. Bad things happen to good people, but we can be 100 per cent certain that God sees everything that happens and He is with us. God sees what you have done and he knows the truth.

You may not have been unfairly accused of attacking someone or thrown into a dark pit by your brothers, but I am sure you can remember times when life seemed unfair. You might have been wrongly accused of taking something that wasn't yours or of being unkind to someone. Sometimes what we say and do can be misunderstood. People may think the worst of us, not realizing that we are trying to be kind.

It is important to remember that God knows. It is important to remember that God loves us and is with us no matter what we go through. If someone hurts you and treats you unfairly, you may not want to forgive them. Jesus forgave the people that killed him. He forgives us for all the wrong things we do. Not only does he forgive us, but he also offers us life in heaven. He can help us forgive other people too. If we don't forgive then the feelings of anger and hurt will hang around us like heavy chains. In a way, we will be stuck in a dark pit or in prison with no joy or hope. It can be hard to forgive people and you may need someone you trust to help you do this.

It is also important to stand up for what is right when we know things are wrong. Today there are more people in slavery than in Joseph's day. It is unfair and it is unjust. Many people are treated like objects and are not valued as they should be. There are organizations that work to stop this happening like 'Stop the Traffik' or 'The International Justice Mission'.

There are many ways in which life can be unfair. Below is a list of things that you can do when unfair things happen to you:

- Talk to people you trust about what is going on.

- Talk to God about what is going on. Trust God.

- Ask God to help you to forgive people when life is unfair.

On the next page is a prayer that you can pray. You may want to say your own prayer or write one down.

Prayer

Dear God,

Thank you for loving me no matter what happens in my life.

Thank you for reminding me that you see everything. When people accuse me of things I have not done, you know the truth. I can trust you. Help me to trust you and to talk to you about what is going on in my life.

Thank you that Jesus died for me. He was accused of things he did not do but he was able to forgive people. Help me to become more and more like Jesus.

Thank you that you love me,

Amen.

Remember, God cares for you even when life is unfair.

This is a space to write your prayers.

CHAPTER SIX

PRACTICAL HELP

for Parents, Carers, and Teachers

One of the most important things we can do
for our children is to help them learn to cope
with the difficulties of life. Stress, sadness, and
disappointments are a natural part of people's
lives. Bad things can happen to good people. If
children learn to cope while they are young, it
means they will have the strength and confidence
they need as they mature. It is important to

explain that life can be unfair. This provides us with an opportunity to discuss how there are injustices in the world and how we can deal with the things that happen to us. This will help our children to become resilient adults.

It is good to focus on what we are thankful for but we need to explain that life may not always be like this. In the world we live in there is unfairness around heritage, ethnicity, poverty, and health. The world is fractured and broken but God knows that. He sent Jesus as a solution to this problem. Good talking points are:

- What was God's plan for a broken world?
- What does that mean for me?
- How do we feel when things are unfair?
- How do we forgive?

We often hear the words, "It's not fair!" from children when they are upset. It can be simply about feeling that they are not treated in the same way as others. Perhaps a sibling has a larger piece of cake on his or her plate.

It is helpful to teach children the difference

between what is fair and what is equal. Beliefs around these concepts can stir up intense emotions. Equal means things are exactly alike. Fair is about decisions that are made based on individual needs. Not all children go to bed at the same time and it is a fair decision when parents decide on a bedtime based on the age of a child. It is helpful for children to see the underlying reasons for such decisions.

Children may also struggle with the idea of injustice or the realization that life is sometimes unfair. It can bring about the same intensity of emotion. They may see something on television or they may be accused of something they haven't done. They may respond just like adults do with heightened emotions of anger, upset, and anxiety. Help them to identify what they are feeling and what has caused this response. You can also discuss the following steps that may help them:

- What is the big picture? Help the child to keep a sense of perspective and not to lose control.
- Help the child to make a plan. Often our first response is to stand up for the underdog,

shout, or get angry about a situation.

- If the child is angry, tell them to close their eyes (this helps to block out what has happened) and to take some deep breaths.
- Once the child is calm, chat about what they can do.

You can help a child to reflect on their feelings and think about what their response will be. Obviously this is also dependent on the situation. The first place to start is asking God for His help. You can also highlight what the child can be thankful for.

Ultimately, remind the child that there are times when we cannot change things but that God is in control. Sometimes we cannot do anything but pray and ask God to change the world we live in. Always end this conversation focusing on God – his love and the hope he gives us that one day things will change.

Resources

Care for the Family:
https://www.careforthefamily.org.uk/

Scripture Union:
https://content.scriptureunion.org.uk/resources-activities

The National Society for the Prevention of Cruelty to Children (NSPCC) have some helpful articles on their website:
https://www.nspcc.org.uk/

Other Books in the Series:

Debbie Duncan, *God Cares When I am Afraid:
Jesus Calms the Storm*
Debbie Duncan, *God Cares When I Don't Give Up:
Jesus and Zacchaeus*
Debbie Duncan, *God Cares When I am Strong:
Friends in the Fire*

9 781 78128 374 5

9 781 78128 404 9

9 781 78128 375 2

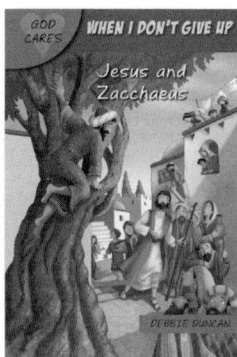

Debbie Duncan, *God Cares When I Am Anxious: Moses and Other Stories*

Debbie Duncan, *God Cares When Life is Tough: Paul and Other Stories*

Debbie Duncan, *God Cares When I Feel Down: Jonah and Other Stories*

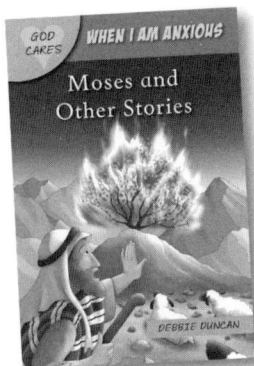

9 781 78128 376 9

9 781 78128 399 8

9 781 78128 377 6

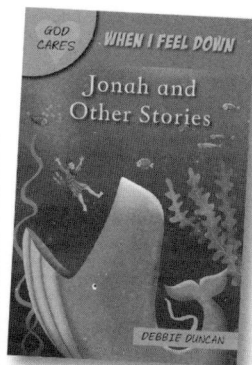